FIRE SEASON

JOSEPH LEASE

chax

tucson

2023

Library of Congress Control Number: 2023946631

First Edition 2023

Chax Press

6181 E Fourth St

Tucson AZ 85711

https://chax.org

On the cover: *The Fate of the Animals*, detail of the
painting by Franz Marc, 1913, now in the public
domain. The original painting is in the collection of
Kunstmuseum Basel, Basel, Switzerland.

For my mother,
Mariam Dubovik Lease

CONTENTS

Part One

RIDING DEATH

(he was wild, a little

wild (he's

dying (you can't

exhale (he's

dying (he's

asking why

you

love him

(riding death (kisses

that we

share across the sky (he

is the drunk lane, the

mayor, drunk lake,

drunk

in the lake, he's so

tired and he can't

(what

(my father just feels Sidney

Bechet, Hart Crane, Krazy Kat

(now he doesn't have any (he

gives life (kisses that we

share across

the sky

(riding death

(the book will save the book

(oil will kill the world (he's just

trying to see, pay attention (he

said

(he said joy

(he said feel this (blue green

voice (he said violet, blue

wind

pushes river light, birches

(riding death

(he's dying in a town

full of rabbits (he's

dying, lying on the

couch

(riding death

(he hates "sentimental slop" (hold his

hand, he's from Coney Island, he's

tougher

than you

(he says, when I squeeze your hand

(I'm squeezing her hand

(his mother in the room (his

mother's me (tell him (tell

him (your mother

loves you (riding death

(branches, paradise (are you blue,

are you green, are you fire, are

you gold (have you come, have you

come, to sing to me, to sing to me

(riding death (drunk like coins, like

coins ("our lifestyle is wrecking the

planet for Christ's sake" (she's

drunk like a gold coin, he's drunk

like a gold coin

(the tv says the tv

(farmers are farmers

(corporations eat them

(rabbits are perfect

(riding

death (ice and the river

(blue night comes

(no, no one (nobody dies

(nobody loses (riding

death

(where is the distance, where are the

gym shoes, where are the toenails,

where is the pain, where are the

toenails, please stop this screaming,

please breathe my newsflash, my

eyes don't fit

(riding death (joy could (blue fire

(torn blue (you (dear one (dear

smart, shining you (dear you (my

father's what (my father's rain

becoming rain (riding death

(soft wind like a road

(done (I wrote done

(I tried to write don't

(don't, don't, don't

PART TWO

IN A FIELD

(I changed the distant language of

the rain (the brown and red leaves in

the autumn gray (I wrote the splin-

tered aspect in the wind (I wrote the

splintered aspect in my mind (I wore

the rain that rose and fell like light (I

wore the snow that piled up by the

gate (I wrote the secret number on

my hand (I write the secret number

in my eye (I thought the thought of

every thought but one (I dreamed the

dream that dropped me in the sun

PART THREE

FALLING

(so yes

(I want to tell your story

(I have to "make it up"

(you tried

to be

joy

(did you tell me your story

(we "forgot" to see

(that's part of it

(you said

(cream light

cream thick

purple

clouds

(the end

of the

world

maybe

(fire clouds

(we

killed the

animals

(fire clouds,

extinction

(once

when

some child

could

draw

your voice

(my

mother (turns

to paper

(dying on

the kitchen

floor

(mom

(the animals

are dead,

are dying

(mom, did

I try

(my mother's face is gone (so

what is real

(maybe sunlight

(my mother's face

(we touch the gone voice

bent in half (and mom is

green and she is dead

and she is

where oh where

(she was

the search

for God

(for love

(the summer

wind

(the starry

night

PART FOUR

NOW WHAT

(and the snow fell (and the passing

clouds (and the windows and doors

(and the snow fell (and we answered

(oh what can you (what are you

(something was happening (night fell

(and broke in a million pieces (the

soft wind (the soft air (night fell and

broke

(and the world fell (I walked in the

trees (in the shadows of the trees (the

world flew (the world flew away (like

light

PART FIVE

EVERYTHING MERGES

WITH THE NIGHT

(it's a dream of the end (the mountain (the sun

(but the world is burning (I don't care what I

know (I feel so sick

(the puritan diaries ("American" self

(maybe I'm a liar (half joke, half damage (rain

pouring down (the big branches move (the

secrets in the gutters (the dream death (the

corpse gives commands (we stay inside our

city (cold city

(cold night (a picture of a thought (a garden

(skyscrapers, empty tombs (soul of bullets (I

was exploding

(everything's corpse light (my mother won't

speak (I tried to be joy (walking home (cold

night (red frozen sky

(spin the night

(will we

kill the

world

(the sky

    (is fire

  (shed

   your

     skin

(did we

kill the

world

(will we

kill the

world

(look

(green water

PART SIX

CRACKED ACTOR

(the soul was a spy, the soul was a forest, the

soul was a shipwreck, the soul was a mouth

("does God love me"

(the new warning is fire in

your

face

(system collapse

(I

thought I

had a

future (I

(I want joy

(I taste poison

(I am the ghost of I, etc. (I was a fool,

I had a plan, and water was my dirty

name, I'm writing inside death, I'm in

the room

(in the sweet exhale of July (where dead

zones pock the mind (just west of the end

of the world (where the local lost boy nailed

dogs to the walls of his shack (where the

headless ghost dogs run through the waste

(and walls of flame (and walls of flame

(you spin the spin, you go insane, you

eat the light, you eat the pain

(fire

tsunami,

birds

on fire

(just breathe

night,

    breathe

night

(forever

(just

say

    drop your

eyes right

    here

("quick,

learn

to die"

(the animals

are dead, are dying *(mom,*

you read the books to me,

and I tried

(my legs are trembling, my hands are

trembling (believe me, don't believe

me, I don't care (I was the future, says

the nothing man (I was the future for

a day or two

Author's Note

This book is informed by the work of the
following writers as well as ongoing events
(environmental devastation and the global
movement toward fascism) and personal ones
(the deaths of my mother and father): Giorgio
Agamben, Charles Alexander, Kate Aronoff,
Roland Barthes, Robert Creeley, Dodie
Bellamy, Jem Bendell, Octavia E. Butler,
Donna de la Perrière, Emily Dickinson, Amitav
Ghosh, Allen Ginsberg, Roland Greene, James
Hansen, Donna Haraway, Stefano Harney
and Fred Moten, Bob Kaufman, Jamaica
Kincaid, Naomi Klein, Elizabeth Kolbert, Hank
Lazer, Andreas Malm, George Monbiot, Toni
Morrison, Anahid Nersessian, Akilah Oliver,
Cynthia Ozick, Donald Revell, Adrienne Rich,
David Shapiro, Ayisha Siddiqa, Rebecca
Solnit, Juliana Spahr, Mark Statman, Greta
Thunberg, David Wallace-Wells, Lisa Wells,
Kathryn Yusoff, and many, many others.

The poems in *Fire Season* try to confront
environmental catastrophe as a way of life,
a way of learning to die, a way of witnessing
and acknowledging personal and collective
responsibility, a way of mourning, and a way
of going on.

Acknowledgements

Grateful acknowledgment is made to the editors of the journals in which these poems first appeared—*The Brooklyn Rail, Interim, New American Writing,* and *The Ocean State Review*—and to California College of the Arts for making the writing of this book possible through the generous awarding of a faculty research sabbatical grant. Overwhelming gratitude too to the many beloved poets whose wisdom and insight made this book what it is, none more than Donna de la Perrière and Charles Alexander.

About the Author

Joseph Lease's critically acclaimed books of poetry include *The Body Ghost* (Coffee House Press, 2018), *Testify* (Coffee House Press, 2011), and *Broken World* (Coffee House Press, 2007). Lease's poems "'Broken World' (For James Assatly)" and "Send My Roots Rain" were anthologized in *Postmodern American Poetry: A Norton Anthology*. Lease's poem "'Broken World' (For James Assatly)" was anthologized in *The Best American Poetry* (Robert Creeley, Guest Editor). His poem "Free Again (Why don't people)" was published in *The New York Times*. Lease's poetry is also collected at *PennSound,* The Poetry Center at San Francisco State University, KQED (NPR), The Scottish Poetry Library, The Poetry Project, *Bay Poetics, The AGNI 35th Anniversary Poetry Anthology, Litscapes 2015, The Colorado Review, The Denver Quarterly, New American Writing, The Brooklyn Rail, Interim,* and elsewhere. Lease has been asked to read at numerous colleges and universities. He has received The Academy of American Poets Prize and numerous grants and awards in poetry and poetics from Columbia University, Brown University, Harvard University, and California College of the Arts. Lease is a Professor of Writing and Literature at California College of the Arts.

I really don't know how Joseph Lease does this. Reaches such lyric heights with such delicacy. With skillful use of anaphora, and perfect, various, open-verse forms transformed page to page, Lease is a tour-de-force master of prosody, of the subtle music of words evoking, in this case, passionate feelings of caring, of grief, of sorrow for this broken world. These poems are unique; nothing I have read is like them.

— Norman Fischer

The poems in Joseph Lease's *Broken World* are as cool as they are passionate, as soft-spoken as they are indignant, and as fiercely Romantic as they are formally contained . . . Lease has complete command of his poetic materials. His poems are spellbinding in their terse and ironic authority: Yes, the reader feels when s/he has finished, this is how it was — and how it is. An exquisite collection!

— Marjorie Perloff

Joseph Lease is a major American poet of our time.

— Maria Damon

The Body Ghost is part of a body of work that is significant and reveals Joseph Lease to be a major force in contemporary American literature.

—Sheila Murphy

Remarkably inventive and evocative work from Joseph Lease, one of the finest poets writing today.

— Michael Bérubé

As a document of suffering and redemptive love, *Broken World* belongs in a long line of modernist texts, Zukofsky's "A", Crane's *White Buildings*, Reznikoff 's *Testimony*. The long sequence "Free Again" has already made itself an essential event, thrillingly anthemic. The release of *Broken World* is one of the signal events in recent poetic history.

— Kevin Killian

One test of a book is how you feel about the writer and his or her work on completing the volume. In the case of Joseph Lease's *Broken World*, I want to read everything he's ever written, and for everything that's written but not yet in print to get published as soon as possible. *Broken World* is a dazzling performance whose only weakness, to my eye and ear, is that it could have been much longer.

— Ron Silliman

About Chax Press

Founded in 1984 in Tucson, Arizona, Chax has published more than 250 books in a variety of formats, including hand printed letterpress books and chapbooks, hybrid chapbooks, book arts editions, and trade paperback editions such as the book you are holding. Chax also creates programs that engage students of literature and of the arts of the book, through classes and workshops. Chax presents several public events each year, including poetry readings, artists' talks, and small symposia on topics of poetics, the arts, and our social culture.

Your support of our projects as a reader, and as a benefactor, is much appreciated.

You may find CHAX at *https://chax.org*

Book Design and Production Management
by Charles Alexander, working closely with
the author.

Fonts used in this book are
Bookman Old Style Pro and Copperplate.

The book is being printed and bound by
KC Book Manufacturing.